## NOTES ON AUTHORS

**Penny Trafford** is a general practitioner, and a course organiser for Barnet GP Vocational Training Scheme. Until recently she was a GP trainer. She began this work when she was a member of Patients as Partners in the Department of Postgraduate General Practice North Thames (West).

**Fedelma Winkler** was the project leader of the Patients as Partners project. She is a fellow of City University Health Management Group. She was Chief Executive of Kent Family Health Services Authority and has worked for community health councils and voluntary organisations.

The Patients as Partners project was set up by Professor Pietrioni, Dean of Postgraduate Education in General Practice, North Thames (West) and was funded by the London Implementation Zone Initiative. The aim was to develop the competencies of a group of primary care workers so that they could take forward public involvement in primary care.

The ideas, criticisms and comments of other members of the group, Tania Eber, Anna McCreadie and Renos Pittarides, shaped this report.

January 2000

# Contents

Appendices

# Executive summary

**PRACTICES FREQUENTLY COMPLAIN** about demanding patients and these patients get categorised into groups. This study has taken one such group commonly perceived as putting stress on practice. It explored the underlying problems and collated available data on the perspective of the various stakeholders. Using this as a base it looked at the changes that could be made to practice organisation to reduce the stress on the practice, enhance care and use the expertise available in the community to contribute to a partnership in care. The aim is to maximise gain for the practice, patients and community.

# Foreword

**THE GOVERNMENT POLICY** toward refugees and asylum seekers has little coherence and can often overwhelm the capacity of local services to provide for this vulnerable group.

General practitioners are often, because of their accessibility, the first line of call for most refugees presenting with complex physical, psychological and social needs. The young girl who has been repeatedly raped and has watched her family tortured and killed, to the university professor fleeing with his family from a repressive regime - will all challenge the most compassionate and organised general practice.

In this time of great change, it is a tribute to British general practice that not only can it provide a sensitive and reactive service but, as is described, it can also develop thought through and proactive support for a group of patients whose culture, language and health care needs are so different from the local communities. None of this can be successfully achieved without the dedication and altruism demonstrated in this book - but just as important is the financial support. Over 100,000 refugees are anticipated to arrive in the UK each year. It is hoped that the national planning agencies will be as responsive, as sensitive and as proactive as Penny Trafford's general practice.

**Professor Patrick C Pietroni**

# Stimulus for Change

An increase in the number of refugees registering with Penny Trafford's practice, in outer London, was the stimulus for this monograph. The practice was unprepared. This fact resulted in practice stress and a sense that good quality care was being compromised. The journey from defining refugees as a problem for the practice to the creation of a service to meet their needs is described here.

The first step was to explore the needs of refugees so that the practice could respond appropriately. Working with the Patients as Partners programme, the approach was broadened. It became a case study in practice development aligned with patient involvement.

Most practices have no problem in identifying a group of patients that causes frustration. One response is to attempt to get the patients to change so that they fit into the practice. A less commonly tried response is to examine how the practice could benefit from adapting its organisation to fit the specific characteristics of the patient groups. This report describes the latter approach. The essence of the approach lies in the examination of the problem from the perspective of all the stakeholders; patients, GPs, receptionists, practice nurses, community groups. It requires an appreciation that the organisation of care is an important component of good care and that practice organisation may need to change.

The case study focuses on refugees and demonstrates the rich repository of information at national and local level to help the stakeholders understand the issues. It shows the amount of good will that is available in the community to resolve difficulties. Sadly, there are relatively few examples of practices using the available information and tapping the goodwill of the community to work together to achieve better services. We hope that this case study will show the rewards of such a way of working.

The methodology used here is applicable to any group defined by the practice as a problem. It is part of the larger Patients as Partners educational programme currently under development at the Department of Postgraduate General Practice North Thames (West).

**Penny Trafford, Fedelma Winkler**

# Understanding the problem: user and community perspective

BEFORE REFUGEES REACH our practices they will have been on a journey not just from their own country but through the bureaucracy of immigration. Staff in practices will know little about this journey, or will have distorted information based on newspaper headlines. Understanding a little about the journey and background of refugees is where primary care workers need to begin their own journey. Unless they do that

> Refugees - includes a person who has left their country owing to a well-founded fear of persecution for reasons of race, religion, nationality, membership of a particular group or political opinion, and who is unable, or owing to such fear, is unwilling to avail protection of that country.
>
> Defined by the 1951, and extended by the 1967, UN Convention

they can not begin the process of engagement with refugee care.

## WHERE REFUGEES COME FROM

Where refugees come from varies and is dependent on where major upheavals are taking place. Normally the majority of refugees will be young males. Refugees and displaced people are increasing in number around the world; the Refugee Council estimates that there are 13 million refugees in the world today. Ninety per cent stay in the surroundings of their own region. The recent upheavals in Europe account for the increase in refugees in Britain. In 1999, 50% more people applied for asylum in Britain than in 1998.

By the end of the 1999 these numbers had begun to drop.

AN ASYLUM SEEKER is someone who has lodged a claim in a country but has not yet been accepted.

Persons with a right to remain are people who have not been granted asylum but have been given a right to remain in a particular country for an agreed period of time, usually four years.

The backlog stands at 90,000. An amnesty was offered to 30,000 who had waited 18 months or more.

In the recent past the largest groups seeking asylum in Britain were from areas covered by the former state of Yugoslavia (Kosovo, Montenegro, and Serbia - 16%) Somalia, (10%) Sri Lanka (8%) and Afghanistan (5%). The average refugee age in 1998 was 26 and 77% were male. Thirteen per cent were accompanied by dependents. In 1998, some 3,000 were unaccompanied children.

The 1991 census of population in Haringey found 81% were under 40, and although some 40% of the refugee population were single those with children had larger families than the local population. Of those with children 40% were single parents. Twenty-five per cent of Somali refugees had four or more children. Kurdish and Saudi households also had many children.

**Table 1 *Gender and age***

---

1991 CENSUS OF POPULATION OF HARINGEY

| Refugees | |
|---|---|
| 81% | < 40 years |
| 41% | single |
| 47% | married |
| 70.2% | living with spouse |
| 23.5% | partner in home country |
| 40% | single parents |
| 25% | Somali > 4 children |

## BEHIND THE STATISTICS

These global statistics hide much human suffering. The single parent households may be divided families waiting for the spouse to join them. They face long and uncertain delays. Meanwhile, they worry about the fate of those they left behind. This is said to be one of the most painful problems the refugee endures. Single parent families have to come to terms with caring for their children on their own in a strange environment. They may be doing this while coping with the aftermath of having seen their spouse killed or not knowing if they are dead.

(Note: Family member is defined as spouse, male dependent children under 18, females under 21)

## DIVERSITY

Different groups of refugees settle in various parts of London. In Camden and Islington, for example, the refugees are predominantly single men. The population will include people with stories that are variants on Hemel's.

Hemel is from Algeria. Since he arrived in the country, he has been sleeping rough and occasionally staying in the mosque in Regent's Park. He is not entitled to any benefits, because he did not apply for asylum immediately on entering the country. He recently discovered that his brother had been killed in a car bomb planted by Islamic fundamentalists. It has devastated him and he has been refusing either to eat or talk. Although the Refugee Council was able to find him somewhere to stay temporarily to help him recover from his brother's death, he is now homeless again and back on the streets.

In Barnet, the refugees are mainly families in their third resettlement. Their stories too are tragedies. The case of Abdul shows how the poverty and isolation at the end of a refugee's journey can compound the problems they bring with them.

Abdul was a petrochemical engineer and the manager of a petrol company in Iran. He was wealthy and married with children. He was taken as a political prisoner, tortured and had his property confiscated. He suffered a cerebral vascular accident. Large amounts of money were paid to various agencies to get him out of Iran. He now lives in temporary accommodation in North London with no financial resources. He speaks little English and is severely disabled and depressed.

Abdul's needs are multiple: physical - related to his blood pressure and stroke; psychological - the aftermath of torture and isolation; social - the unsuitability of his housing for someone with his disability, and finally his poverty.

## THE REFUGEE JOURNEY

What happens at each stage of a refugee's journey affects their health status. The stages have been categorised as:
1.      Pre-refugee situation
2.      Displacement period
3.      Initial response - arrival at camp
4.      Travelling to long term settlement country
5.      Settlement as refugee in host country
Rifat's story illustrates the enormity of the psychological trauma refugees may bring from their home country.

Zoran and I are Serbs from the same village in Bosnia. We were childhood sweethearts and we were married at 18. Soon we had three beautiful children, we worked hard and every dinar went to building a good home for our family. One morning I went to pick some fruit, on my way back I called to my children - there was no answer. Slowly I pushed the kitchen door open. Zoran and my three children were lying on the floor; they'd been shot and their throats cut. Later I heard they'd been killed by the Muslim Blackshirts from the next village. After that, I couldn't stay in Bosnia. So, now I'm in London. I know that all I have left is a photograph, I have no past, no present, and no future either.

An appreciation of the first four stages and the physical and psychological complications are important for giving adequate care.

Health is often not the refugee's first or main concern. There is the initial problem of getting asylum status which can involve long questioning and paper work. For those with children it is an easier process. Until asylum status is granted there is the fear of deportation as well as the danger of exploitation and the dependency on friends or on poorly resourced voluntary organisations. Local authorities differ in the arrangements they make to provide accommodation and food.

## REFUGEES IN BARNET

In 1996, Barnet Refugee Health Access Project did a needs assessment exercise (see Appendix 1) to develop a proactive programme to improve refugee access to health care and to support practitioners in providing appropriate services to the refugee community.

They contacted approximately 150 refugees by means of focus groups, questionnaires, casework, and through discussion with refugee community groups. The social characteristic of refugees in Barnet reflected the national profile. Most had families larger than the Western average. This caused accommodation problems. Housing in London is designed for small families so overcrowding is common and aggravates stress-related health problems.

**Table 2 *Number of children living in families of questionnaire respondents***

| No. of children in family | 1 | 2 | 3 | 4 | 5 | 6 | 7 | 8 | 9 | Unknown |
|---|---|---|---|---|---|---|---|---|---|---|
| No. of families | 12 | 6 | 9 | 7 | 4 | 3 | 1 | 0 | 1 | 2 |

Single mothers who are separated from their partners headed many of the families. The partners were still in refugee camps abroad or were unable to join them for legal/political reasons. This situation aggravates problems, especially depression.

The survey highlighted the children's problems. Many come from countries where they have had no formal education and feel alienated and stressful in an unfamiliar environment. This is manifested in behavioural problems which schools found difficult to manage. In some cases the schools lacked the resources or the motivation to identify solutions. At others they lacked an understanding of the situation. The children and schools experience language problems, which creates further alienation between themselves, their teachers and peers.   Children's problems can be compounded by parents' inability to see their suffering because of their own grief and despair.

**Table 3 *Age range of refugee children***

| Age of children Under | 2 | 2-4 | 5-10 | 11-16 | 17+ | Unknown |
|---|---|---|---|---|---|---|
| No. of children | 5 | 8 | 42 | 41 | 22 | 18 |

The survey identified a problem with finding schools.  Some schools did not have space.  Others, as mentioned above, did not have the resources to respond to the special needs of refugee children.  The schools which are willing to accommodate refugee children and their problems, often necessitate lengthy travel to reach them.   These problems are similar to those experienced by refugees when using health care.

### 'FAIRER, FASTER, FIRMER'

The new Immigration and Asylum Act will come into force in April 2000.  Under the Act asylum seekers are forbidden to work to support themselves.  They will receive vouchers to exchange for goods.  They will be housed in nine regions where there is housing available. These arrangements will be foreshadowed in the emergency scheme that came into effect in December. It aims to relieve pressures on councils in Dover and London and to spread the load more evenly around the country. Approximately 300 applicants a month will be dispersed.

Single people will be allowed £10 per person in cash each week. There is no limit on the proportion of support that can be given as cash to asylum seekers with children.

### PATIENT DEMAND

In the next section the issues are explored from the perspective of general practice.  The demands on a practice reflect where the refugees come from and the stage they have reached in the refugee process as well as the socio-demographic characteristics of the group. Above all they reflect the circumstances that drove the refugees from their own country. In addition to the trauma of their background, once here they share the problems of the socially excluded; poverty, poor housing isolation and difficulty of access to services.

Users and deliverers of services see problems differently. If we are to ensure that the patient experience is central to good care it is important that we examine services from their perspective.

# Not understanding the problems: practice frustration

**COMMUNITY GROUPS FREQUENTLY** carry out surveys of problems in their area. These surveys are often attempts to quantify problems that have been brought to them. The style of general practice is usually determined by the practitioners not the patients. Practices seeking to understand the problems their patients face in using their services will find helpers in community organisations. This section draws on the work of Barnet Refugee Health Access Project, which had documented the problems practices in Barnet experienced when caring for refugees. Through personal stories it attempts to put those problems in context.

## ISSUES OF COMMUNICATION

Good communication is vital to effective primary care. It is hindered when culture and language are different.

*In order to provide health care which is appropriate to the needs of the population of a general practice, GPs have to consider not just the symptoms and signs of illness, but the role of social and cultural factors in its origin, presentation and treatment.*[1]

Lack of a common language was the biggest barrier to care identified by the practices in their responses to Barnet Refugee Health Access Project Survey. This led to other problems. Time was an important consideration when deciding to register refugees. Consultations that involve an interpreter increase the length of the consultation so refugees needed longer appointments. The consultations are also more demanding because of the multiplicity of problems that had to be addressed. Fifty per cent of the practices surveyed found this an issue.

In all, 28 practices (74%) said the practice had problems when offering services to the refugees. The practices' biggest need was for interpreters. In the survey 22 practices (58%) used interpreters, many of these were family members. Sixteen per cent used link workers, although many practices said these were often not available when needed. Five doctors were multilingual and one practice used a staff member for interpreting. The GPs wanted more money to care for refugees.

An increase in interpreting availability and an education programme for refugees on the Health Care System were the practices' solution to the problem. Neatly this requires no change from them.

## IS IT DISCRIMINATION?

Refugees attributed their difficulty in registering with practices to discrimination. Refugee organisations complain that refugees are registered as temporary patients even when they are settled in a practice area. They put this down to racism. The practices meanwhile said they accepted refugees as permanent patients. These differences illustrate the lack of dialogue between the practices and the community groups.

GPs have scant knowledge of the refugee situation. Practices assume refugees have knowledge of how the health care systems work. The reality is that the refugees may have been introduced to the NHS by a practice with a very different culture. They may have registered initially with a practice without any appointment system. Yet the next practice expects them to turn up when they do not need to see a doctor. Practices may fail to understand that mobility is forced on refugees and that this may be a factor in their failure to keep appointments.

## PRACTICE NEEDS

Staff and refugees bring very different expectations to the consultation. Practices described a variety of problems they experience. Sixteen practices (42%) which responded to the survey remarked on the incidence of anxiety and depression among the refugees. They felt ill equipped to treat because of their own lack of expertise and the inadequate support facilities available. The unavailability of social service advice and difficulty in getting counselling for torture victims was a concern. Refugee patients also involve the GP in form filling or letter writing to obtain benefits, housing or other related issues.

Lack of a shared understanding of health and health care between practices and refugees caused further problems. Practices say that refugees turn up to register when they needed to see the doctor. This often leads to lengthy and frustrating exchanges with the receptionist. The consultation that follows is inadequate, confined to dealing with acute problems. With insufficient time or organisation to record the past medical, social and family history, all of which may be complex, the doctor becomes frustrated and the patient receives inadequate care.

Turning up late or not at all and failure to keep hospital appointments annoys practices. So too does the low priority refugees give to preventive health, such as childhood immunisations and health promotion. The frustration is shared by practices at all stages of development.

Amina's story gives a human face to these difficulties. It illustrates the lack of understanding of health care by refugees and the failure of health care to adapt to the refugee's situation.

> In April 1993, Amina, a 16 year old, non-English-speaking Somali refugee, came to see one of the general practitioners because she had started to experience fits. The GP noted that she had been treated for active tuberculosis two years previously, but the correspondence appeared to have stopped mid-treatment. It emerged that her family had

been moved - refugees are normally housed in temporary accommodation and so move about frequently - and as she had appeared better, having changed address and GP, she was lost to follow-up. By now Amina was seriously ill, with a cerebral tuberculoma causing the fits. She was referred back to the hospital and fortunately, after 18 months of intensive therapy, she has now recovered.

In summary the barriers to health access are communication, information, and practice organisation. The components of each of these barriers are isolated in the diagram below. Each of these components needs to be addressed to overcome the problems.

# **3** Clinical background to refugee health care

**RATES OF INTERVENTION** vary between different communities. These variations can not always be correlated with the incidence of disease in the sub-population. Although the structural problems relating to communication and resources should be addressed, more detailed comparative studies of the care received by patients from different ethnic groups needs to be undertaken to assess the full extent and nature of the problem.

Variations in health status between different ethnic groups are assumed to correlate with socio-economic status. An approach which ignores socio-economic position and uses ethnicity as a surrogate indicator of socio-economic status is unacceptable.

To address the needs of refugees, primary care staff have to understand why refugees present with problems. To cope adequately with the care of refugees professionals need to familiarise themselves with key elements in clinical care. These are outlined this section.

## KEY ELEMENTS IN CLINICAL CARE

### Physical

Many physical problems are similar to those of the general population but factors such as malnutrition, poor hygiene and associated infections, injuries related to traumatic experience and female genital mutilation must all be considered during health checks.

Many refugees and displaced people are psychologically traumatised. Some may go on to develop mental illness. The degree of help needed has to be individually assessed. Refugees are not prone to seek help from mental health services and the effects of stigmatisation have to be considered.

## HEALTH PROBLEMS

# Children

*Physical*
Constant and recurring upper respiratory infection
Fever and flu-like symptoms
Eczema, skin complaints and allergies

*Psychological*
Fear, sadness, sleep disorders,
psychosomatic complaints/regressive behaviour,
irritability, restlessness
apathy, lack of interest, mistrust, lack of self-confidence,
poor concentration, learning difficulties.

Not included in the above are children who arrived in this country already with varying
degrees of physical and mental disability.

# Women

Recurring headaches
Depression
Upper respiratory tract infections
Skin diseases, eg psoriasis
Gynaecological and hormonal problems
Pre- and post-natal health monitoring
Musculo-skeletal debilities
Nutritional depletion manifested by dental and
skeletal ailments

# Men
*others –*

*Each of the following has a knock-on effect on the*

Anxiety and depression
Isolation
Loss of self-esteem
Mental disorders, such as aggression
Dependency on chewing khat which then exaggerates
the problems listed above but also creates psychological
and physiological disorders which can be misdiagnosed
by medical practitioners as a pattern of schizophrenia eg:
Inability to sleep
Constipation
Loss of appetite
Anxiety
Aggression, which can lead to violence

HIV/AIDs in all three categories

*Information compiled from focus groups with refugees Barnet Health Access Project*

## Psychological

The term *post-traumatic stress disorders* covers a spectrum of traumatic disorders, ranging from the effects of a single overwhelming event to the more complicated effects of prolonged trauma and repeated abuse. Examples of these disorders are:

- the rape trauma syndrome
- the post-concentration camp syndrome
- the combat-related traumatic stress syndrome

The salient characteristic of a traumatic event is the power to inspire helplessness and terror. The main symptoms of post-traumatic stress disorder involve hyper arousal symptoms, intrusion of memories, and constrictive symptoms. Because post-traumatic symptoms are so persistent they may be mistaken for enduring characteristics of the victim's personality.

People subjected to prolonged, repeated trauma can develop an insidious, progressive form of post traumatic stress disorder (the syndrome of chronic trauma) which invades and erodes the personality even further. They begin to complain not only of insomnia and agitation, but of numerous types of somatic symptoms.

An increasing problem is drug abuse amongst refugees. In Barnet, at the Drug and Alcohol Service, there is a counsellor specialising in drug abuse. It is possible that some resort to drugs to obliterate their feelings and experiences.

## DIAGNOSIS

The key to successful treatment is correct diagnosis. Particular problems are:

### A. Depression

This may present as:

- changeable and vague pains
- gas stomach, chest or head (physical tension)
- generalised body weakness (anergia, loss of interest)

### B. Psychosis

The problem with dealing with other cultures is usually overdiagnosis:

- Paranoia: complex and systematised delusions can be recognised at once, but where there is only an expression of grievance and victimisation it is more difficult in the context of inequality and discrimination.

- Delusions: beliefs which seem to the doctor to be erroneous and bizarre, and therefore delusional may be quite normal eg belief in magic.

- Acute reactive stress-induced psychosis: rarely amongst indigenous British subjects does stress produce psychotic symptoms, but in other cultures an acute reactive psychosis is more commonly diagnosed. These patients may be too readily diagnosed schizophrenic.

## FAMILY REUNION

Families get separated as they flee persecution. They may not know what has happened to family members they left behind. The not knowing and the striving for contact or to be reunited puts great stress on refugees. Almost all refugees coming to the UK can expect very long delays before their family joins them. The regulations preventing family reunion are felt by refugees to be the greatest and most painful problems they must endure as they rebuild their lives.

## WOMAN REFUGEES

Rape is frequently used to persecute women either as a weapon of war during armed conflict or to torture women who have been detained. Women can also find themselves the victim of other forms of degrading or inhumane treatment. In some countries beatings and whippings are used to punish women who do not confirm to dress codes or attempt to work or study.

Some refugee women are trying to cope not only with their pre-migration trauma, but also with separation from their husbands (alive or dead) and with being a single parent in an unfamiliar country.

## CHILDREN

Children of refugee families are all scared by the changes occurring in their lives, are experiencing important losses and many are deeply

traumatised.
The most frequent symptoms portraying the emotional reactions of
refugee children are:
fear, sadness, sleep disorders

then:
psychosomatic complaints, irritability, restlessness,
aggressive/regressive behaviour

leading to:
apathy, lack of interest, mistrust lack of self confidence, poor
concentration, and learning difficulties.

Some parents do not see the suffering of their children. Others do,
but because of their own grief and despair they may lack the energy
to help their children.
Poor social support and lack of an extended family for emotional
support are strong predictors of depression. Therefore to alleviate
this, planned, integrated rehabilitation programmes and attention to
social support and family reunion are important.

It is the interaction of the physical and the psychological, complicated
by the cultural interpretation, that makes the provision of good care
to refugee patients a challenge in terms of both clinical care and the
way the practice is organised.

## BARRIERS TO HEALTH ACCESS

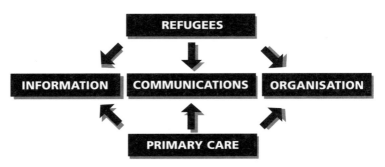

# Organisation within practices

**THE MULTIPLE AND** complex clinical and social problems which refugees bring to the practice have been outlined. Too often practices lack appreciation of these problems and this lack of understanding is exacerbated by not sharing a language. To some practices refugees are just another group of demanding, time-consuming patients. To others their problems are overwhelming and staff feel inadequate and ill-prepared to cope. In this section, the ways three practices responded to refugee patients are explored.

## FIRST PRACTICE: REACTIVE CARE

The first practice visited was in the centre of a large, newly arrived refugee population. The patients were mainly single young men living in bed and breakfast accommodation and this practice was, for many, their first contact with the NHS. It was a long-established, single-handed practice that employed an assistant doctor and reception staff. It had a practice nurse and had attached community nursing staff.

The practitioner perceives his practice population as having changed from respectable white working class to one largely of refugees and other transient people. In contrast to his 'old' population he defines them as high users of service. He also perceives a change in attitude from respect for the doctor, who had cared for families over generations, to demanding patients who want instant care. On one sample evening 14 out of the 21 patients seen were refugees; the majority did not speak English.

The practice did not have an appointment system. There were no staff speaking other languages and no language cards were used. The practice does not recognise in its staffing or organisation that most of its patients could not speak English. Patients were seen on a first come first seen basis. The practice perceived the refugees as knowing their rights but not how the NHS system worked.

All the patients requesting registration were accepted and most were registered as temporary patients. Registration was a difficult process for the receptionist and was conducted with extreme irritation. The staff had no special training in communication across language barriers.

A high volume of work plus a constant stream of new patients can lead to strained relationships and unfulfilling work in the best organised practice. The lead practitioner complained of the conflict between the practice and the community interpreters and other support workers. The support workers wanted the practice to have appointment times so they could arrange to attend with patients or with a group, but the practice said there was no point because the patients came and demanded treatment when they needed it.

To the outsider the practice was a battleground. The practice was attempting to stay in control and maintaining their traditional way of working seemed to have become the source of satisfaction. If a patient wanted to see a doctor then they had to do so on the practice's terms; accommodating others' needs was giving in to others' inappropriate demands. The practice did not adjust its organisation to reflect the health profile of its current population.

The practice was not under pressure to develop services in line with needs from anybody other than the refugee support workers. This pressure was dismissed and seemed counterproductive. No additional resources had been made available to the practice by the health authority to enable it to change.

## SECOND PRACTICE: PROACTIVE CARE

The second practice visited was in central London where many refugees, both single people and families, were registering.

This practice had organised two refugee clinics a week, run by a nurse practitioner with extended consultations, and team working with Social Services plus voluntary organisations. These had been set up to ease the burden on the practice. The success of this scheme seemed highly dependent on the nurse practitioner who was about to leave. Although there was a serious attempt to work together, the refugee workers perceived the practice as not owning the clinics and that they had too little involvement from the general practitioner.

## THIRD PRACTICE: THE NEED TO CHANGE

In Barnet, by the time refugee patients register they are on their second or third practice - the result of the rehousing policies. There were rarely more than two refugee patients per surgery; they were mainly families, often a lone partner, with large numbers of children in their third settlement. They had experience of using the NHS. The problems the Barnet practice was experiencing were minor in comparison with the first practice. Yet the problems experienced had similar foundations.

To achieve a satisfying consultation GPs need to listen to and understand the patient's problems. This means conducting an appropriate examination, verbal or physical, according to the information gathered, and then with the patient formulating an action plan. With the refugee patients this was impossible: there was rarely an interpreter available so consultations were begun with little knowledge of the refugees' history, culture, or family life; there was insufficient time to record the medical, social and family history, all of which could be complex; there was not enough time to unravel problems; and the initial contact was inadequate as it was reactive and dealt only with the acute problems. This resulted in dissatisfied and uncomfortable GPs falling at the first hurdle.

It was not just the GPs in the practice who were frustrated and had problems; outside at reception pressure was obvious. There was no consistency in the way the receptionists responded to the refugees' request for registration. Sometimes a distinction was made between refugees and asylum seekers; on occasions they would ask for passports and documentation. The inability to get details from the refugee caused aggravation.

The nurses had other problems. The patients invariably arrived for the first time wanting to see a doctor. Once the acute problem was dealt with they failed to return for their appointment with the nurse. The new registration checks were largely unattended, which was very wasteful of the nurses' time, particularly when a family had been booked. The GPs had to struggle to get the information during a consultation - an inefficient use of their time. All these problems resulted in the refugee patients, despite their neediness, in the practice's view, getting a less than adequate service.

### PRACTICE ORGANISATION AND PATIENT NEED

The first practice exhibited the hallmarks of what Irvine and Irvine (Table 4) describe as a traditional practice. The second practice sought to meet its needs by establishing a separate clinic but had not kept all its stakeholders involved. The third practice sees itself as a modern practice seeking to provide planned care that reflected patients' needs but it had failed to apply these criteria to this group of patients.

Two of the practices expressed great frustration. In both, the tensions were obvious. The third had off-loaded the tensions. The situation was unsatisfactory. In one the lack of an appointment system was restricting access to interpreting help; in the other, despite appointments, interpreting help was rarely available. In the proactive practice the refugees were not conforming to the practice's expectations of patients any more than they were in the traditional practice. They didn't fit into either organisation.

**Table 4 *Movements in general practice***

| Traditional practice | Modern practice |
|---|---|
| Reactive care | Planned care |
| Individualism | Teamworking |
| Provider focus | Patient focus |
| Personal responsibility | Collective responsibility |
| Implicit (variable) standards | Explicit standards |
| Single model | Flexible provision |

The Practice of Quality: Donald and Sally Irvine

The policy of dispersing refugees from London to the regions will mean that many practices will be in the situation of the third practice. The challenge is to find ways that the special needs of specific definable groups can be met in a way that enhances the satisfaction of those providing care. Therefore, beyond understanding the problems of the group the practice organisation has to be reviewed to identify where it needs to be adjusted. Unless the staff feel supported and the system works for them and for the patients optimum care is not possible. Systems also have to be put in place for collaboration with the specialist agencies and gaps identified so that those with responsibility for rectifying them can be alerted.

# **5** Meeting practice and refugee needs

**PRACTICES RECOIL WHEN** asked to develop services tailored to the needs of a specific group. It is vital, therefore, when considering change, to examine how the life of the practice can be enhanced while providing a better service to patients. That is the philosophy that underlines this section.

## THE LANGUAGE BARRIER

### INTERPRETATION

It is the inability to communicate which causes most problems to practices. Improving access and care is dependent upon improving communication. This is not a difficult problem to solve.

Telephone interpreting services are available up to 24 hours. This links doctors immediately with a telephone interpreter. While this can be a cumbersome three-way conversation, simple technology such as speakerphones can significantly aid the consultation. Some organisational rearrangement may be necessary to ensure consultations with non-English speaking patients take place in consulting rooms with speakerphones.

Many health authorities employ link workers who may be available to general practice to act as interpreters. Each practice ought to be familiar with the arrangements within their own area.

Responsibility for contracting with the interpreting service needs to be agreed locally. If health authorities do not have suitable arrangements then GPs will need to put pressure on the primary care groups to contract for such a service.

Using interpreters will mean changes in working habits and the acquisition of new skills such as working through a professional interpreter. The incentive is the reduced frustration that ensues and satisfaction from giving appropriate care.

## USING INFORMAL INTERPRETING
In general practice heavy reliance is often put on informal solutions. A family or friend may be brought along to interpret. This can lead to problems. The most obvious is that while the informal interpreter may speak English their comprehension may be poor and further distortion can occur because of the emotion or delicacy of the situation.

These problems are magnified in cross-gender and cross-generation interpretation. Rack[2] states that 'under no circumstances should children be asked to interpret medical details for parents. It appears to us unethical, unprofessional, uncivilised and totally unacceptable'. There are situations when a family member interpreting for children may also be unacceptable.

The use of informal interpreters is inappropriate and possibly counterproductive when seeing people with mental health problems. An interpreter who is emotionally involved with the patient is likely to intrude their opinions and interpretations (consciously or not) into the translation. This is particularly damaging when psychosocial factors or interpersonal problems are part of the problem.

There may be situations when the use of informal interpreters is appropriate or inevitable. Guidelines to help decide when and how to handle informal interpreting will help staff and patients and should form part of training.

## WORKING WITH INTERPRETERS

Introducing interpreters into regular use requires changes in administrative procedures, training to make effective use of them and adjustments to the practice so that they can be involved as part of the team.

The practice has to ensure that the patient's facility in English is recorded. If this is poor, the language spoken must be included in the registration form. This information can be used to arrange for interpreting when appointments are made. The value of recording language needs to be incorporated into the receptionists' training.

Fuller and Toon[3] warn of drawbacks when using interpreters. The interpreter may leave out a vital piece of information, may not understand a word or concept, may put in their own advice, interpret what they think the doctor wants to hear or become angry or impatient. If the practice has involved the interpreter in discussions and built up a relationship these problems are reduced. Training in getting the best from interpreters needs to be incorporated into service training.

Training has to include guidance on working with both formal and informal interpreters so those drawbacks are minimised. Staff need guidance in judging when professional interpreting is essential. On occasions the involvement of a family member may be appropriate just as it would be for any patient. In some cultures it is unthinkable that family members would not be involved in care. It is important that refugee patients are not treated differently from other patients just because they do not speak English.

As part of planned care interpreters and/or advocates should be included in discussions about practice arrangements and organisation. Specialist voluntary organisations can be involved productively in these discussions.

## COMMUNICATION ACROSS LANGUAGE BARRIERS

Because there are always situations when getting interpreting help will not be possible it helps if staff are trained to communicate with people who speak little or no English, or who speak English as a second language:

Mares[4] suggested practical ways in which doctors can improve communication. These include:

1.  reducing stress  - by pronouncing name correctly, plenty of non-verbal reassurance, allowing more time, writing down important points clearly for the patient to take away.
2.  simplify your English - (avoid patronising) speak clearly and slowly, use words the patient is likely to know and simplify form of sentence, give instructions in logical sequence, stick to one topic at a time.
3.  checking back properly - get the patient to explain back what they are doing.

Guidance and practice in using different kinds of interpreting needs to be incorporated into training programmes.

## USING LANGUAGE FACILITY OF STAFF

In some areas there are GPs, nurses or other members of the primary health care team who are bilingual. If staff language facility is to be used regularly it has to be a part of planned care and recognised as part of their job. Special training may be needed.

Where there are many refugees from particular areas, appointing a receptionist who can speak a relevant language may be beneficial.

Some refugees are professionally qualified and competent in the English language. They find it very difficult to get employment in their professions. When recruiting staff, applicants might be sought from amongst the refugees.

Many health care staff have worked in the troubled areas from which refugees come; they are a valuable resource. Voluntary organisations that recruit staff for overseas assignments can help with contacting returning staff.

## RECOGNISING CULTURAL CONTEXT

Expectation of health care depends on health beliefs that are influenced by individual, educational, socioeconomic and cultural aspects. Unless health beliefs are considered we may not meet the need of individual patients.

Practices who offer services to refugees have an obligation to familiarise themselves with their particular needs and problems. Culture and custom influence all communities. Communities are homogeneous and generalisations should only be made with care. The cultural influence on medicine and health has to be incorporated into training of staff.

Particular areas of consideration are:
1.    Explanations - care should be taken to make sure that explanations and instructions are understood
2.    Holistic approach - practitioners from other cultures often include advice about what the patient and family can do themselves, diet, sleep, sexual activity, environment etc
3.    Some treatments may be more familiar and better received than others
4.    Delay in effectiveness of medication eg antidepressant pills abandoned

## PRACTICE DESIGN AND ORGANISATION

## RECEPTION AND REGISTRATION

Reception staff are important to good care and must be included when planning services. They are rarely trained in working across cultures and with people who do not speak English. Frequently they do not understand why the refugees are coming into the area yet they are the first contact with the practice. Some problems arise because they are unsure about the rights of patients to register with the practice. The practice must ensure that they have clear guidance on whom to register and the category of registration.

## PRACTICE POLICY ON TEMPORARY REGISTRATION

Refugees are re-housed frequently during their initial adjustment. This can justify their registration as temporary patients. Even in areas where they are more settled refugees are apparently not always offered permanent registration. This may be because practices perceive refugees as an increase in workload and therefore the higher reimbursement is seen as compensation for this increase.

This can be detrimental to continuity of care since temporary patients are only registered for three months. The practice needs to have an agreed policy on registration and guidance for staff; it should not be left to the receptionist on duty. There are other implications. If the refugees are expected to move out of the area consideration needs to be given to patient-held records. Refugees are very aware of the importance of documents. This aids continuity of care and ensures that resources are not wasted on re-doing patient profiles.

Practices registering significant numbers of refugees may need help for extra staffing, additional resources for health promotion or for services offered at the practice such as psychological stress clinics. Accurate records on language and length of stay and practice policies will aid the practice in obtaining additional resources.

---

### RIGHTS TO NHS TREATMENT

All refugees, asylum seekers and those with exceptional leave to remain have the right to be registered with GPs and receive prescriptions free of charge.

They also have the right to hospital care if the meet the conditions of residency. At hospital they are asked the following questions:
.           Have you been living in the UK for the past 12 months?
.           On what date did you arrive in the UK?
.           What is the basis of your stay in the UK?
As refugees are in the UK for the purpose of resettlement there should be no problem in providing answers to establish eligibility to the NHS.

For those no longer receiving Income Support following the introduction of the Asylum and Living Act 1996, there is only exemption from charges for:
.           prescriptions
.           dental treatment and checks
.           sight tests and NHS glasses
.           fares to hospital for NHS treatment
by obtaining an HC1/2/3 exemption certificate

HC1        Claim for Health Costs
HC2        NHS Charges Certificates for Full Financial Help
HC3        NHS Charges Certificates for Limited Financial Help (for those who have some regular income or financial savings).

Those asylum seekers on vouchers, ie not receiving benefits, must fill in form HC1 in order to get free prescriptions. Until this form is processed, which takes several weeks, they are liable for prescription charges which they may not be able to afford.

---

## REGISTRATION FORMS AND COLLECTION OF DATA

Each practice decides its own criteria for registration. Sometimes there are difficulties at the reception desk in gathering basic information. There is variation in questions asked and they may be interpreted as intrusive (at least) or racist (at worst). A patient registration questionnaire smoothes the interface (see Appendix 2 for example questionnaire).

## NEW PATIENT CHECK

All patients are offered new patient checks. Comprehensive information gathered at this stage shortens the consultation with the GP and enables the health needs of the individual to be more effectively met.

See Appendix 3 for a template developed for use during the new patient checks undertaken by the nurse. A longer consultation enables the patient to establish a relationship with the nurse and, through the nurse, with the practice. Problem areas can be identified for referral to GP or other specialist attention. These sessions with the nurse are crucial. They can improve refugees' understanding of preventive health measures, particularly childhood immunisations. They also ensure that the refugee understands how to get the best from the service offered.

Certain issues will not be fully dealt with in the first consultation. No one is likely to reveal the traumas of hardship or torture or some of the migratory stresses in the first consultation. The new patient health checks undertaken by a nurse trained in understanding the problems of refugees and with the help of a trained interpreter can ease the stress and ensure appropriate services are offered.

Audit is important in order to decide what information is appropriate for the nurse to collect. When on a template it should be easy to assess the pickup rate of, for example, HepB/HIV if blood tests are done.

## FORMS AND LETTERS
GPs are reluctant to register refugees because they think it will involve them in excessive form filling. These forms and letters are associated with applications to charities for grants, letters to official bodies to support claims for war injuries, welfare claims such as for maternity grants, help with transport and income support.

An audit of such requests suggests that they are not significantly greater than for other groups. The initial health check should enable some administrative work to be completed on registration, saving frustration and delay later.

## HUMAN RESOURCES
Organisational structures will have limited effect without staff trained to deal sensitively with refugees. The character, performance and quality of the human resources needs to be reviewed.

Issues:
1. Language and communication capabilities.
2. Diversity in staff group.
3. Understanding of cultural issues.
4. Discussion of racism at the possible different levels; interpersonal, organisational/institutional and the structural/societal levels.
5. Examination of non-clinical issues and proposed organisational changes.
6. Examination of clinical issues.
7. Effective team working.

## SEGREGATION AND INTEGRATION

Some people have advocated separate health care for refugees. Arguments are made for the establishment of centres with special expertise. Refugee workers are loudest in their advocacy of separate specialist services. This arises from their difficulty in getting refugees registered with GPs.

Specialist services may be a solution in first settlement areas where there are concentrations of refugees. The settlement policy is to disperse refugees to centres around the country. It is not, therefore, always practical to establish separate services.

## SPECIALIST REFUGEE CLINICS

The appropriateness of special clinics depends on the number of patients from similar groups and the range and type of problems they are bringing to the practice. In some areas it may be appropriate to develop the special services jointly with other practices or with the local NHS Trust or specialist community group.

Specialist refugee clinics need to have an enlarged team, including link workers and voluntary or community organisation workers. Members of the team need to value each other's contribution and have a shared understanding of potential and function. Team building is crucial when planning, funding and setting up services for refugees.

Staff training needs to be undertaken across the whole primary care team, combining staff development, language and cultural training.

Actions:

1. Training on cultural differences and specific health needs.
2. Training involving Refugee Council/local refugee project workers/voluntary organisations etc.
3. Training on how to work with interpreters.
4. Courses: internal to practice

   local refugee forum/consortium organisations eg London Interpreting Course, St Bartholomew's Health Advocacy Care.
5. Training for working with new organisation, within practice.

---

SPECIALIST REFUGEE CLINICS WITHIN GENERAL PRACTICE

Setting: - In the practice
- Regular weekly clinic(s)

In a multi-ethnic area, working with voluntary organisations the advocate/interpreters present varies on different weeks.

Appointments:
- Extended appointments
- 1st consultation 40 minutes
- Subsequent consultation 20-40 minutes

Staff: - Run by nurse or nurse practitioner
- Receptionist
- Link workers/interpreters present
- Voluntary organisations:
   - may provide link workers/interpreters
- Mental health
   - Counsellors either through voluntary organisation or
   - Community NHS Trust

Tasks: - receptionist undertaking registration (more easily done at this time)
- counselling
- health visitor advice for children and elderly
- voluntary organisations:
   - provide information/leaflets (multi-lingual)
   - advice on benefits etc
   - networking
   - personal support to individuals/families
- nurse 1st consultation - new patient check; undertake blood tests if policy agreed by practice
- emergency consultations; flexibility within system for emergencies if nurse practitioner available. The interpreters would then be available. If doctor needed, GP consultation would take less time because problem(s) already identified.

## APPROPRIATE PRACTICE DEVELOPMENT

The practice wishing to offer proactive care to its refugee patient has to examine each aspect of the practice's organisation, administration and staff development and training programme. This section outlines the issues that need to be addressed. It suggests pathways for practices to explore. Ways forward can not be prescriptive but ought to be reflective of the numbers of refugees and the stage of their resettlement. They must also reflect the practice capacity for development.

Adaptation should be compatible with the needs of the practice so that change can bring a sense of well being to the practice and result in better care for patients.

# Refugees and Practice Development

**THIS SECTION DESCRIBES** the process of converting the information gathered and applying the theory to the practice. It describes the politics of project development: an initial failure to secure funds may later prove successful if the project bid is ready and the constituency primed.

## MATCHING NEED TO SERVICE

Much of the literature on needs assessment stops with the identification of need and the problems of meeting that need. Recent articles on the Government's dispersal programme are good examples of this approach.[5,6]

The challenge of this project was to explore the relationship between needs assessment and the services provided. A long list of needs can be daunting and overwhelming, and sometimes the demands made by refugees can cause frustration. The aim, therefore, was to examine how the practice could integrate refugee care and meet their needs, whilst also improving the functioning of the practice. It was not enough to introduce interpreting services, other areas had to be addressed, eg ensuring that forms were filled in correctly required administrative staff to understand why and to adjust their procedures.

Applying the 'Patients as Partners' approach, the Barnet practice began examining each of its own procedures. The willingness of the practice to explore solutions meant that the local refugee group was pleased to help.

The receptionists and the nurses contributed to the development of the registration forms and the new patient health check. These changes made a significant difference to how refugee patients were perceived. The introduction of a registration protocol meant less confusion and led to fewer alterations, which also reduced the receptionist's anxiety.

Whilst checking the practice leaflet in preparation for translation, its limitations for English speaking people was highlighted; it needed to be rewritten before it could be translated.

Understanding the resources available in the community enabled the practice to get help. The health authority link workers were able to provide an interpreting service, and the practice receptionists understood the importance of this service and how to organise interpreting. The improved communication helped the refugees to understand how the practice works and the importance of the consultation with the nurse. However, the problems of people not attending continue and require further analysis. Contact was also established with the Mental Health Trust and proposals for a special counselling clinic developed.

Training has been in the form of discussions at the GP/receptionists' meetings, but staff training in association with the refugee group is also being discussed. The recent appointment of a black and ethnic minority worker by the health authority will, hopefully, enable training to be organised at district level in the future.

A proposal for an integrated service that brings together health, social services, housing, legal and the voluntary agencies at the community hospital was submitted to the health authority's Health Improvement Programme (HImP). Under this proposal, practices would continue to register refugees but could ask the centre to do an extended health check following the agreed template. The information would then be fed back to the practice with refugees returning to their own practice for care, ensuring integration into primary care.

The proposal was not successful - out of the three primary care groups in the area only one supported the proposal. The West Locality Primary Care Group was in favour of the initiative, believing it valuable to its patient population and the GPs trying to work with refugees. The South Locality Primary Care Groups already had a different model working at Homeless Action in Barnet. The North Primary Care Group did not support the idea as refugees are not numerous in its area and therefore it was not perceived to be a priority.

However, a bid was made by the West Locality Primary Care Group for a nurse-led Primary Care Centre (PCC) at Edgware Community Hospital, which also included a proposal to set up a specialist refugee clinic (see Appendix 4). This bid proved successful.

In order to obtain Government funding the PCC must be operational by April 2000. This time scale makes it a difficult task; the refugee service will need to develop more slowly to ensure involvement of all the contributors to the partnership.

Barnet Health Access for Refugees plans to relocate to the centre, which means that in addition to the refugee clinic there will also be people on site to help with walk-in refugee patients.

Before setting up the refugee service, the education of staff within the centre is seen as crucial. Study days for all staff are planned using the expertise of the Medical Foundation for the Victims of Torture.

In the future, it is planned to extend this training to GPs and their staff throughout the area. In this way the PCC will become an education centre for primary care teams.

# 7 Working with the Community

PRIMARY CARE HAS been slow to tap into community resources, to involve the community and to work with them in order to achieve common goals. The voluntary contribution of practice staff to the community is rarely built on or recognised within the practice. The team, patients and the wider community can benefit when practices work with community organisations.

The obstacles to implementation are usually the lack of energy and time. Traditionally, practices reacted to patients' demands but gradually there has been a shift to proactive, planned care. The same shift needs to take place regarding community initiatives. This means applying the principles of modern practice to working with the community - planning for involvement, involving voluntary organisations in the team, being open about how we work and being clear about our contribution.

## USING LOCAL RESOURCES

Support for refugees relies heavily on voluntary organisations and volunteers, but such organisations are a resource rarely used by practices. They can help practices recruit volunteers, inform the refugee community about services and encourage understanding between the practice and the community. A rota of volunteers can be set up within the practice.

Many voluntary organisations have written leaflets for refugees that give information about general practice. These leaflets have been translated into numerous languages. Practices identify the important need to inform and educate refugees, yet they rarely make use of existing material. Voluntary organisations may also be willing to translate a simplified practice leaflet, they will know of material already translated and can advise on what information is most needed. It may be easier for the practice and the voluntary organisations to collaborate when raising funds to pay for translation rather than working independently. Jointly informing and educating patients can improve the practice's efficiency as well as establishing co-operation within the community.

The practice, for its part, has to be aware that voluntary organisations can replicate the political factions of communities and this can affect their acceptability to patients. Practices need to be sensitive to refugee politics and it is 'umbrella' organisations that can usually help practices understand local tensions.

Refugees arriving in a new area can feel very isolated as they don't have knowledge of local support agencies and thus, find it difficult to get help. The practice can play a pivotal role in linking refugees to these support agencies. In order to do this one individual needs to act as the liaison person and be responsible for maintaining an information database on local sources of help.

The practice can alert the social agencies to small refugee groups with no organised support so that gaps in services can be identified and local groups alerted.

The local council for racial equality or the local community health council can advise on groups in the area and simplify the development of partnerships. Some areas will have refugee consortia or networks. Information directories are usually available from one of these organisations. In Barnet the Refugee Health Access Project were very willing to share information, provide support and work in partnership. What is crucial is a practice's willingness to invest in developing these mutually beneficial relationships.

## VOLUNTEER ORGANISERS

There is guidance for practices wishing to have a volunteer coordinator.[7] Examples of practical help organised by practices include: befriending; bereavement counselling; sitting; and the development of carers/toddlers/mothers groups; prescription collection/shopping. Transport to and from medical appointments is often a particular problem for asylum seekers.

One practice-based person needs to have responsibility for liaison but individual staff may take responsibility for different groups. Having this link can bring new expertise and knowledge to the practice and enable it to offer services well beyond the remit of statutory provision. The link can be a volunteer with designated responsibility and accountable to a member of staff.

The need for extra statutory services is not specific to refugees. However, practices may find it easier to set up a volunteer scheme with a particular focus. If a practice has a volunteer scheme in place already, it may need to be reviewed so as to ensure it is sensitive to the needs of specific groups such as refugees.

Recruiting an organiser is crucial but not necessarily difficult. What is important is that the practice has given thought to the parameters of the scheme and the support they are willing to offer. Within the community, there is always a fund of goodwill and skill and a great deal has been published on the use of volunteers in Third World countries. Throughout the Third World national governments have placed great importance on village health workers and volunteers who serve as the interface between formal health care systems and the local community. Here, people who retire early or who work part-time are often prepared to volunteer their skills. The local volunteer bureau is available for advice.

## REFUGEES AS CO-WORKERS

Refugees are a vulnerable group: isolated, separated from a family network, homeless, single parent families, many with social and psychological stresses. Such a needy group may be unable to commit themselves to a process of patient involvement in practice or at community level. It is necessary to work with advocates and voluntary groups to ensure an effective voice. Part of their care may involve helping them to help others - refugees who have been through the system welcome being able to help others.

Often, the professional qualifications of refugees are not recognised. If practices are open and sensitive, professionally qualified refugees can be given opportunities to participate in educational programmes and to contribute to discussions.

## PRIMARY CARE GROUPS (PCGS)

Primary care groups offer new opportunities to think about the needs of special groups. Discussions need to cover the appropriateness of designating practices to develop specialist services. Organisationally, this could be similar to out-of-hours co-operatives. In some areas, practices are already experimenting with offering services to neighbouring practices. One practice could be funded to develop services for the refugees in the neighbourhood, whilst other practices could target the needs of other groups, such as the severely mentally ill.

These arrangements require a high degree of co-operation amongst practices and strategic management from the PCG. They also require the PCGs to share information and resources with community organisations.

Voluntary and community groups, while willing to help and be involved, have financial restraints. The PCGs must consider how they will commission work and monitor take-up.

PCGs are allocating resources to meet the requirements of public involvement. Lack of finance and administrative resources has been a factor in preventing individual users and user groups becoming involved, leading to under representation by disadvantaged groups. Representatives from the refugee community could play a larger part in health service policy, planning and purchasing if a small investment was provided towards support, prior briefing, explaining of committee procedures and there was consistent practice on travel expenses.

There also needs to be investment in programmes to prepare primary care groups and practice staff for working in partnership with the community (because of the poor history of such previous partnerships). This case study grew out of one such programme.

# 8 — Beyond the refugee community

"**THE GOVERNMENT IS** committed to building a health service which is responsive and sensitive to the needs of patients and the wider public".[8] To achieve such a goal requires staff to understand those needs and how they can be met. Staff, also, have needs, part of which is knowing they are giving a good service. This monograph has tried to find ways in which service users' and service deliverers' needs can be met.

Health professionals and support staff within the relevant agencies do not fully understand what it means to be a refugee, nor do they understand the needs of refugees. Equally, refugees do not understand how the health system works and they learn to use the system in a piecemeal way. This inevitably leads to barriers that prevent the delivery of appropriate care. In this case study the components needed for barriers to be broken down were identified as:

Information and training
> This would take the form of a comprehensive information pack/training video.

Referral/notification system
> A structured referral/notification system that would encompass the journey that a refugee must take to contact services.

Interpreting resources
> This includes training for staff in the use of professional interpreting, informal interpreting and telephone interpreting.

Practice organisation aligned to needs of practice and refugees
> A practice that adjusts its organisation in the light of changing

demand can ease the sources of conflict and meet its own needs better, as well as those of its patients.

Groups seen as the most demanding by GPs are often those with the poorest health status or intractable problems. The organisation of practices is usually best suited to a patient population that is undemanding, healthy or acutely ill. A practice visited as part of the Patients as Partners project had recognised practitioners' inadequacy in coping with the complexity of patients' problems. The stress on them of trying was the motivation for the practice to rethink the way they worked. Using upside-down thinking, they created an infrastructure providing support to staff coping with demanding patients. This led to the practice specialising in patients with intractable problems.

The practice also opened itself to the community to find help and resources for patients and staff as well as community development. This case study sought to apply those lessons to one specific group of patients. A group of demanding patients were selected, their needs explored, and ways were sought that would support practice staff in meeting those demands. Through meeting the demands there is also the potential for staff to grow.

| DEMANDING PATIENTS - UNRESPONSIVE PRACTICE | |
| --- | --- |
| What is the demand? | To whom? |
| Specific needs | Physical<br>Psychological<br>Socio-economic |
| Ways to address problem | Gather information<br>All stakeholders<br>Review of practice<br>Responsibility<br>Training |
| Resources | Available literature<br>Goodwill<br>Community practice |

The methods used can be applied to any group of patients. It is vital to begin with understanding the problem, to use the information available to view the problem from the perspective of all the stakeholders: patients, their representatives, staff, partners. Teasing out the problem and who it affects is crucial. Then there is the need to explore the untapped resources and goodwill in the community that can be employed to help resolve the problem.

Finally, it is essential to get the commitment of the whole practice and make time to apply the learning to the practice. That is a continuous journey.

# Appendices

Barnet Borough Voluntary Service Council Refugee Health
Access Project
Responses to Health Professional Questionnaire

1.    Are there refugee patients registered with your practice?
       YES                                                        35
       NO                                                          3

Comments:
       Lots of refugees from Somalia, Bosnia, etc               4
       Lengthy consultations, therefore cannot take too many   1
       African, Sri Lankan                                      1
       No separate records kept to see if refugees              2

2.    If yes, what type of registration does your practice
       offer to refugees?
       PERMANENT                                                35
       TEMPORARY                                                17
       ONE-OFF                                                   3

Comments:
       Some GP surgeries offer different types of registration
            dependent upon different criteria:
       Presume permanent residency                              1
       Offer temporary registration until formalised status

|  | with Home Office received | 3 |
|---|---|---|
|  | Depends on length of stay | 4 |
|  | Permanency equals resident for more than 3 months | 1 |
|  | Dependant upon list vacancies | 2 |
|  | Based on NHS rules | 1 |

3. What health problems do they consult for?

|  |  |
|---|---|
| Multiple | 19 |
| Frequent attendees for viral infections | 1 |

Questionaire

| General health problems | 8 |
|---|---|
| Anxiety/depression emotional | 16 |
| Cardiac | 1 |
| Respiratoral/coughs/asthma | 5 |
| Paediatric | 1 |
| Mental health | 3 |
| Don't consult for psychiatric problems | 1 |
| Psychological/post traumatic | 4 |
| Acute problems | 1 |
| Bereavement | 1 |
| Duodenal ulcers | 1 |
| Backaches and general aches and pains | 3 |
| Insomnia | 1 |
| Diabetes | 1 |
| Anaemia | 1 |
| Hypertension | 1 |
| Long-standing untreated illness | 3 |
| Contraception | 3 |
| Eye problems | 1 |
| Skin problems | 2 |
| Potts disease | 1 |
| Behavioural problems in children | 1 |
| Social problems - housing, schools, disability allowances | 8 |
| Don't know | 1 |

4.  Are there any problems that your practice encounters when offering services to refugees?

|                   |     |
| ----------------- | --- |
| YES               | 28  |
| NO                | 4   |

Comments:

| | |
| --- | --- |
| Language/communication | 27 |
| Late for appointments/don't turn up | 4 |
| High visit rates for minor medical problems | 2 |
| Home visit demands | 1 |
| Frequent attendees | 1 |
| Can't afford prescription charges | 1 |
| Need clearer guidelines re NHS and refugees | 4 |
| Dealing with social issues/housing | 6 |
| Consultations take longer/demands on time | 4 |
| Lack of expertise re refugees | 1 |
| Torture victims need support; counselling | 1 |
| Demands difficult to meet | 1 |
| Demanding/rude/insulting/threatening behaviour | 3 |

5.  If so, describe the problems your practice faces when offering services to refugees.

| | |
| --- | --- |
| 'Demanding their rights', eg instant referral | 3 |
| Language/communication | 16 |
| Certificates to obtain benefits | 1 |
| Cultural differences especially re women | 4 |
| No idea of health systems | 3 |
| Time taken for appointment 5/recording medical history | 2 |
| Lack of social worker | 1 |
| Inaccessibility to social services | 1 |
| High users of NHS | 1 |
| Non-attendance at antenatal clinics | 1 |
| No record of child immunisation | 1 |
| Social problems outside the remit of the NHS | 1 |

Very demanding towards receptionists      1

6.     Do you make use of interpreters?

     YES      22
     NO      9
     NO because speak several languages      5

Comments:

| | |
|---|---|
| Occasionally | 1 |
| When available | 6 |
| None available | 5 |
| Come with an English speaker | 5 |
| If available, interpreters have been excellent | 1 |
| Interpreters booked and then have cancelled | 2 |
| Through link workers | 2 |
| Child of patient | 1 |
| Difficult to get patient to bring interpreter | 1 |

7.     Where and how do you access interpreters?

| | |
|---|---|
| Family/friends | 16 |
| Staff | 1 |
| Young family members | 3 |
| Health worker | 2 |
| Link workers | 3 |
| Refugee agency | 1 |
| Local hospital - Edgware General, Wellhouse Trust, Royal Free | 8 |
| FHSA | 4 |
| Local network | 1 |
| Social services | 2 |
| List of interpreters | 1 |
| Waiting room | 1 |

8.     What provisions do you need to facilitate Health Service provisions for refugees?

Interpreters      10

| | |
|---|---|
| Better interpretation/advocacy | 1 |
| More time | 4 |
| Money | 4 |
| Advice/access to social services/housing | 7 |
| Health visitors/social workers | 5 |
| Research into refugee expectations of Health Service | 1 |
| Education for refugees re health service | 1 |
| Refugee status clarification | 1 |
| In and outpatient accessibility in hospitals | 1 |
| Counsellors/services for victims of torture | 2 |
| Understanding by refugees that they have no priority | 1 |
| Central point of contact for refugee services | 1 |
| Education for refugees re minor illnesses | 1 |

9.  What recommendations can you make to improve the accessing of health services by refugees?

| | |
|---|---|
| Link workers/language facilities | 10 |
| Education for refugees of NHS systems | 9 |
| Leaflets in refugee languages | 5 |
| Use of health/social workers for initial contact | 3 |
| More money for time and staff | 5 |
| More information on who to treat | 1 |
| Placing refugees in areas with doctors who speak their language | 1 |
| Special health centres in areas of high refugee population | 3 |

| | |
|---|---|
| Health Education for refugees | 1 |
| Mental health services | 1 |
| Counsellors from refugee backgrounds | 1 |
| Refugees should bring their own interpreters | 1 |
| Nursery provisions | 1 |
| Encouragement for more politeness and less aggression | 1 |
| English lessons (prior to housing in community cf Netherlands) | 2 |
| Have no problem accessing services | 1 |

## APPENDIX 2

NEW PATIENT REGISTRATION QUESTIONNAIRE
(IF YOU LIVE PERMANENTLY IN THE UK JUST ANSWER
QUESTIONS 1-4)

1  Have you a GP in this area?          Yes/No (please delete)

2  How long have you been in this country?
   From birth            ................................... (tick)
   Year of arrival        ................................... (number of years)
   If less than one year,
     month of arrival     ...................................(number of months)

3  Your country of origin?          UK ..................
                                         EU ...................
                                         Other ...................
                                       (please give the name)

4  What language do you speak?          ........................
   Would you need an interpreter?          Yes/No (please delete)

5  For what purpose is your stay:  (tick one)
     ●          student         .......
     ●          work            .......
     ●          holiday         .......
     ●          refugee/asylum seeker  .......
     ●          Other             .......

## APPENDIX 3

REFUGEE SCREENING TEMPLATE

STATUS          FULL
                TEMPORARY
                APPEAL
                ELR
                INDEFINITE LR

YEAR OF ENTRY INTO UK              ..............................
COUNTRY OF ORIGIN                 ..............................
LANGUAGE SPOKEN                   ..............................
NEED FOR AN INTERPRETER           Yes/No

MARITAL STATUS          - married
                        - single parent family
                        - single
                        - other

HOUSING - temporary     EMPLOYMENT        Yes/No
        - permanent     BENEFITS          Yes/No
                        VOUCHERS          Yes/No

INFECTIONS:             Malaria
                        TB
                        Parasites/Worms
                        Hep A,B,C
                        HIV

GENETIC SCREENING:      Thalassaemia
                        Sickle Cell

COMMON SYMPTOMS: eg headaches/fatigue/dizziness/depression
TORTURE
POST TRAUMATIC STRESS DISORDER

## REFERRAL TO OTHER AGENCIES

## MEDICAL RECORDS

Problems:
- no previous medical records
- difficulties because of communication in obtaining PMH
- duplication (by a number of practices) because of high mobility
- Date of birth
- computer system names - name entered computer system western way, forename/surname. Frequently middle name most important and computer labels do not come out in correct order
- statistics: No. of refugees in practice
  language/religion

Solutions:
- Recording at registration:
  - . country of origin
  - . refugee status
  - . religion
  - . language spoken
  - . need of interpreter
- Computer system
  - . includes all above therefore able to get practice profile including refugees
  - . uniformity in way of entering names
  - . Date of birth (best approximation)
- Hand-held records

  To prevent duplication at various practices hand held records would be appropriate. Refugees value their papers and keep them safe. Medical records would be viewed in the same way. The future with computers is obviously hand-held smart cards.

## APPENDIX 4

Proposal for refugee clinic at Edgware Community Hospital

Background

Barnet HA has recommended in their Health Improvement Programme, *Black and Minority Ethnic Health*, the setting up of a one stop service for refugees and asylum seekers.

Barnet Refugee Health Access Project (BBVSC) conducted a needs assessment for refugees in 1996. On 4/6/98 they invited interested parties to meet, and it was agreed to set up the Barnet Refugee Forum and proposed a 'One Stop Shop' be set up.

Penny Trafford, GP Watling Medical Centre, has been working with the Postgraduate Dept of GP N Thames Region on a project Patients as Partners and written a paper, *Refugees and Primary Care: Developing Service to Meet Needs*. In it she includes the development of refugee clinics.

Barnet perspective

GPs in the West Locality Primary Care Group (ie Burnt Oak, Hendon, Colindale, Edgware, Mill Hill), which includes a designated Deprived Area, have been struggling to meet the primary care needs of the influx of refugees in the past ten years.

Edgware Community Hospital with its new information centre and facilities would be ideally placed to proved a One Stop Shop/Clinic to meet the social, financial, legal, physical and psychological needs of all refugees in this locality.

## REFUGEE CLINIC/ONE STOP SHOP

Setting -
Edgware Community Hospital

- regular weekly clinic(s)
- ? different weeks/days different ethnic group

Staff - receptionist

- nurse/nurse practitioner
- link worker/interpreters
- voluntary organisations     Barnet Refugee Health Access
  Project ethnic community
  groups voluntary workers

- SS homeless/refugee and asylum unit workers
- counsellors (Napsbury Ethinic Minority Health Officer to
  facilitate appropriately trained counsellors)
- legal/advice staff
- HV specialist in refugee work

Appointments

- Drop in arrangement, client may wish to see any of staff
- Appointments for nurse and counsellor. Both need extended
  approx 45 min appointments with interpreter present
- Liaison between voluntary groups and clinic
- Liaison between GP surgeries and clinics. Refugee registers
  at practice and then practice phones to make an appointment
  at refugee clinic where nurse undertakes New Patient
  Check plus extended Refugee Template (see attached)
- Nurse
  a) undertakes New Patient Health Check and extended
      Refugee Screening Check for any GP practice
      within area

b) other health advice
Patients would then be directed back to their own GP for routine consultations. The collated information about each patient would be sent to the practice to be entered into their record system so enabling a more pro-active consultation next time, the GP taking up appropriate issues and other staff from refugee clinic already dealing with their specialist areas.

(The proposal of no GP on site is to ensure that refugees are integrated into primary care and will attend their nearest chosen surgery.)

- Health visitor with specialist interest in refugees and asylum seekers giving appropriate advice

- Counsellors with specialist interest in refugees and knowledge of torture and post-traumatic stress disorder. May also need to include family therapists (or? within appropriate hospital or community department).

- Voluntary organisations welcoming? taking on task of receptionists, befriending, support, guiding on to other services. Networking through Barnet Refugee Forum information and liaising with information centre.

- Homeless persons and refugee unit giving advice

- Other taskes to be considered:
- legal advice
- health promotion working with Health Promotion Unit HA
- education of primary care staff
- audit

FINANCE

To be discussed with Barnet HA. The suggestions in this proposal are not core GMS work.

Use non-core GMS monies to be directed to West Locality Primary Care Group?
Pilot study from Health Improvements Programme monies?

BACKGROUND PAPERS

1.   *Needs Assessment 96* Barnet Refugee Health Access Project (BBVSC)
2.   *Health Improvements Programme* Barnet Health Authority
3.   *Refugees and Primary Care: Developing Service to Meet Needs* Penny Trafford MRCGP


Penny Trafford MRCGP
12/9/98

## APPENDIX 5

### Further Reading

Aday, Lu Ann (1994) Health Status of Vulnerable Populations. *Annual Review Public Health* 15: 487-509.

Ahmad WI (1993) *Race and Health in Contemporary Britain.* Oxford, OUP.

Bernard-Jones S (1993) *Haringey Refugee Development Project: Review Document.* New River Health Authority.

Budack N (1993) *Health Needs of Kurdish Refugees in Haringey.* New River Health Authority.

Cruikshank JK and Beavers DG (1989) *Ethnic Factors in Health and Disease.* Sevenoaks, Wright.

Dick B (1984) Diseases of Refugees: Causes effects and control. *Trans Royal Society of Tropical Medicine and Hygiene* 78: 734-741.

Eccles K ( 1996) *Primary Health Care for Black and Minority Ethnic People: A GP Perspective.* Department of Health NHS Executive.

Edwards N, Ciliska D, Halbert T, Pond M (1992) Health Promotion and Health Advocacy for and by immigrants enrolled in English as a second language classes. *Canadian Journal of Public Health* 83(2): 159-162.

Karmi G (1992) Refugee Health. *BMJ* 305: 205-6.

McAvoy BR and Donaldson LJ (Eds)(1990) *Health Care for Asians.* Oxford, OUP.

Mohamed Lul Ahmed (1993) Final Report by the Somalia Health Worker on Health and Somalia Community. New River Health Authority.

Nazroo J (1997) *Ethnicity and Mental Health Findings from a National Community Survey.* London, Policy Studies Institute.

Pietroni P & C (Eds) (1996) *Innovation in Community Care and Primary Health: the Marylebone Experiment.* London, Churchill Livingstone.

Ramsey and Turner (1993). Refugees Health Needs. *British Journal of General Practice* 43 (376): 480-1.

The Refugee Council Factfiles.

## RESOURCES

Barkham P (1999) Beginner's guide to the refugee crisis 27/08/1999
www.newsunlimited.co.uk/Refugees_in_Britain/
This site has links to other relevant sites.

NHS Executive (1999) Patient and Public Involvement in the *new* NHS.

Home Office (1998) *Fairer, faster, and firmer: a modern approach to immigration and asylum. London.*

The Refugee Council has launched an information service to help health and local authorities identify needs and what refugees are entitled to:
Tel: 020 7820 3042

'Patients as Partners' programme Tel: 020 8962 4680;
Email kcyrus@tpmde.ac.uk

# References

1. Helman C. Culture, *Health and Illness*. Bristol: Wright, 1984.

2. Rack P. *Race, culture and mental disorder*. London: Tavistock, 1982.

3. Fuller JS and Toon P. *Medical Practice in a Multicultural Society*. Oxford: Heinemann Medical, 1988.

4. Mares P. Improved Communication. *Health and Race* (1988); **4**: 1-5.

5. Jones D, Gill PS. Refugees and primary care: tackling the inequalities. *BMJ* 1998; **317**: 1444-1446.

6. Hogan H, Matthews P. Meeting health needs of asylum seekers. *BMJ* 1999; **318**: 671.

7. Goodrick I, Nisbett M, White D (eds). *Goodwill in Practice: The GP Volunteer Handbook*. London: Royal College of General Practitioners, 1997.

8. NHS Executive. Patient and Public Involvement in the *new* NHS. London: Department of Health, 1999.